PLANETS

JUPITER

Alexis Roumanis

LET'S READ

AV²
BY WEIGL™

ADDED VALUE • AUDIO VISUAL

www.av2books.com

AV² provides enriched content that supplements and complements this book. Weigl's AV² books strive to create inspired learning and engage young minds in a total learning experience.

Your AV² Media Enhanced books come alive with...

Audio
Listen to sections of the book read aloud.

Video
Watch informative video clips.

Embedded Weblinks
Gain additional information for research.

Try This!
Complete activities and hands-on experiments.

Key Words
Study vocabulary, and complete a matching word activity.

Quizzes
Test your knowledge.

Slide Show
View images and captions, and prepare a presentation.

... and much, much more!

Go to **www.av2books.com**, and enter this book's unique code.

BOOK CODE

Y446263

AV² by Weigl brings you media enhanced books that support active learning.

Published by AV² by Weigl
350 5th Avenue, 59th Floor New York, NY 10118
Websites: www.av2books.com   www.weigl.com

Library of Congress Cataloging-in-Publication Data

Roumanis, Alexis, author.
 Jupiter / Alexis Roumanis.
    pages cm. -- (Planets)
 Includes index.
 ISBN 978-1-4896-3284-5 (hard cover : alk. paper) -- ISBN 978-1-4896-3285-2 (soft cover : alk. paper) -- ISBN 978-1-4896-3286-9 (single user ebook)
-- ISBN 978-1-4896-3287-6 (multi-user ebook)
 1. Jupiter (Planet)--Juvenile literature. I. Title.
 QB661.R68 2016
 523.45--dc23
                              2014041517

Printed in the United States of America in Brainerd, Minnesota
1 2 3 4 5 6 7 8 9 0 19 18 17 16 15

022015
WEP081214

Project Coordinator: Katie Gillespie Art Director: Terry Paulhus

Weigl acknowledges Getty Images and iStock as the primary image suppliers for this title.

JUPITER

CONTENTS

What Is Jupiter?

Jupiter is a planet. It moves in a path around the Sun. Jupiter is the fifth planet from the Sun.

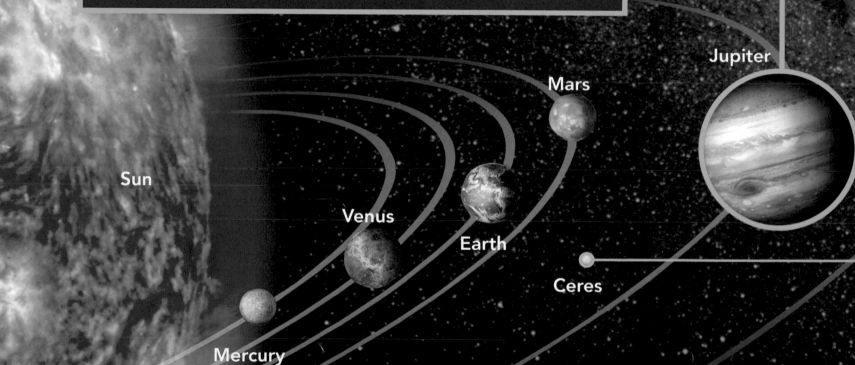

Sun

Mercury

Venus

Earth

Mars

Ceres

Jupiter

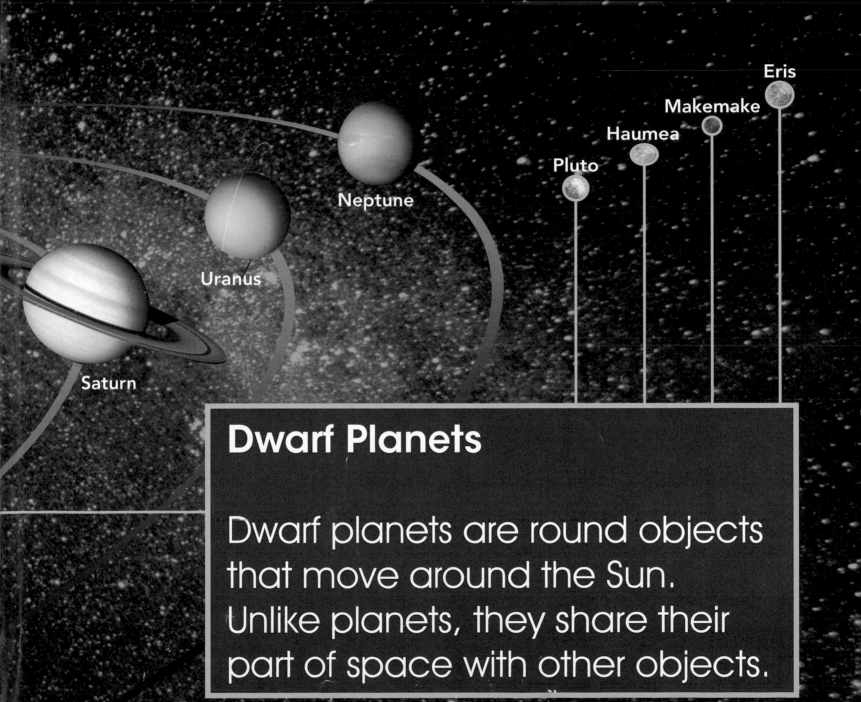

Eris

Makemake

Haumea

Pluto

Neptune

Uranus

Saturn

Dwarf Planets

Dwarf planets are round objects that move around the Sun. Unlike planets, they share their part of space with other objects.

How Big Is Jupiter?

Jupiter is the largest planet in the solar system. It is more than 11 times wider than Earth.

Jupiter

Earth

7

What Is Jupiter Made Of?

Jupiter is a gas giant. It is not made of rock like Earth. Jupiter is made up of fast-moving gases.

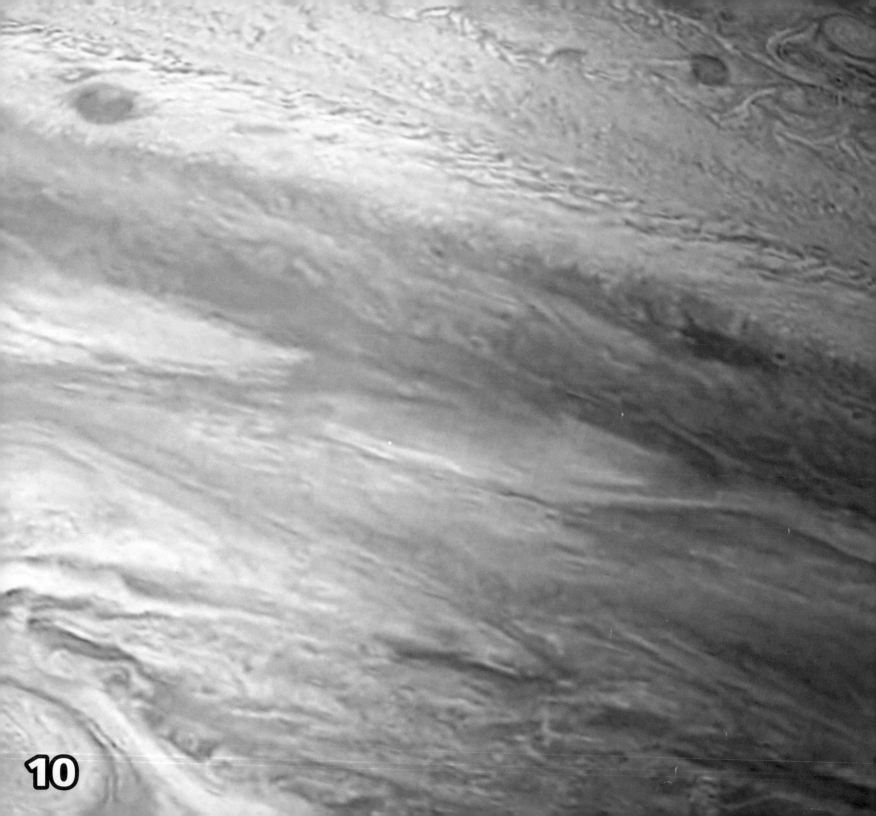

What Does Jupiter Look Like?

Jupiter looks like it has stripes. These stripes are gas clouds. Gas clouds make orange, yellow, white, and red lines around the planet.

What Is the Great Red Spot?

Jupiter has a Great Red Spot. It is a large storm that is twice the size of Earth. The Great Red Spot has lasted for more than 300 years.

Europa

Io

Callisto

Ganymede

14

What Are Jupiter's Moons?

Jupiter has 50 known moons. One of Jupiter's moons is the largest in the solar system. It is called Ganymede.

Ganymede

Who First Studied Jupiter?

The first person to study Jupiter was called Galileo. He used a telescope to see Jupiter and its moons.

18

How Is Jupiter Different from Earth?

The main difference between Jupiter and Earth is size. Jupiter is more than 1,000 times the size of Earth.

How Do We Learn about Jupiter Today?

Scientists send vehicles called probes into space to study the solar system. A space probe called *Juno* was launched in 2011. It will begin to study Jupiter in 2016.

JUPITER FACTS

This page provides more detail about the interesting facts found in the book. They are intended to be used by adults as a learning support to help young readers round out their knowledge of each planet featured in the *Planets* series.

Pages 4–5

Jupiter is a planet. Planets are round objects that move around, or orbit, a star, with enough mass to clear smaller objects from their orbit. Earth's solar system has eight planets, five known dwarf planets, and many other space objects that all orbit the Sun. Jupiter is 484 million miles (778 million kilometers) from the Sun. It takes 4,333 Earth days for Jupiter to make one orbit around the Sun.

Pages 6–7

Jupiter is the largest planet in the solar system. Gravity is a force that pulls objects toward a planet's center. The force of gravity on Jupiter is more than twice as strong at it is on Earth. A 100-pound (45-kilogram) object on Earth would weigh 253 pounds (115 kg) on Jupiter.

Pages 8–9

Jupiter is a gas giant. Most of the visible clouds on Jupiter are made up of ammonia, with unknown chemicals creating orange, yellow, white, and red colors. An atmosphere is made of gases that surround a planet. Jupiter's atmosphere is mostly hydrogen and helium. Some scientists believe Jupiter has a solid core that is about the size of Earth.

Pages 10–11

Jupiter looks like it has stripes. The gas clouds around Jupiter can move at speeds of up to 400 miles (644 km) per hour. Like the planet Saturn, Jupiter has rings of rock that circle around the planet. These three rings are very dark and cannot be seen with an ordinary telescope. The rings were discovered in 1979 during the National Aeronautics and Space Administration's (NASA) Voyager mission.

Jupiter has a Great Red Spot. It is sometimes visible from Earth through a telescope. The Great Red Spot is similar to a hurricane. The storm has lasted for hundreds of years, as there is no solid surface to slow it down. The Great Red Spot is so large that Earth could be placed inside it twice and there would still be space left over.

Jupiter has 50 known moons. Astronomers have also discovered 17 provisional moons around Jupiter. The four largest moons are Ganymede, Europa, Io, and Callisto. Ganymede is larger than the planet Mercury. Scientists believe that Europa has twice as much water as Earth. Io has the most active volcanoes of any body in the solar system. Callisto is covered in many craters.

The first person to study Jupiter was called Galileo. Jupiter shines so brightly that people have recorded seeing it in the night sky since ancient times. When Galileo Galilei began to study Jupiter, he discovered the planet's four biggest moons. In 1610, he noticed that the moons orbited Jupiter. This observation helped him argue that the planets did not orbit Earth, as people once believed.

The main difference between Jupiter and Earth is size. Jupiter has 318 times more mass than Earth. After the formation of the Sun, most of the leftover material went to form Jupiter. The planet is so large that it is twice the size of all the other planets in the solar system combined.

Scientists send vehicles called probes into space to study the solar system. *Juno* will reach Jupiter in July 2016 and enter a polar orbit, where it will remain for one year. Its mission is to study how Jupiter was formed. *Juno* will use solar panels to power its onboard science instruments. It will also see below Jupiter's dense clouds for the first time. *Juno* will map Jupiter, providing experts with data that will help them to better understand the planet and the solar system.

KEY WORDS

Research has shown that as much as 65 percent of all written material published in English is made up of 300 words. These 300 words cannot be taught using pictures or learned by sounding them out. They must be recognized by sight. This book contains 56 common sight words to help young readers improve their reading fluency and comprehension. This book also teaches young readers several important content words. These words are paired with pictures to aid in learning and improve understanding.

Page	Sight Words First Appearance
4	a, around, from, in, is, it, moves, the, what
5	are, of, other, part, that, their, they, with
6	big, Earth, how, more, than, times
8	like, made, not, up
11	and, does, has, lines, look, make, these, white
12	for, great, large, years
15	one
16	first, he, its, see, study, to, was, who
19	between, different
21	about, begin, do, learn, we, will

Page	Content Words First Appearance
4	Jupiter, path, planet, Sun
5	dwarf planets, objects, space
6	solar system
8	gases, gas giant, rock
11	clouds, stripes
12	Great Red Spot, size, storm
15	Ganymede, moons
16	Galileo, person, telescope
21	*Juno*, probes, scientists

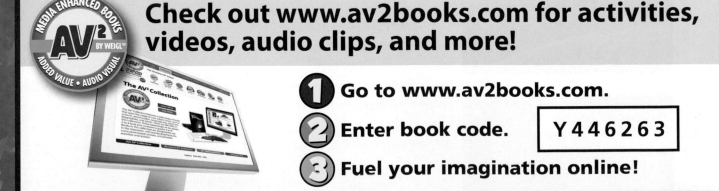

MEDIA ENHANCED BOOKS
AV²
BY WEIGL™
ADDED VALUE • AUDIO VISUAL

Check out www.av2books.com for activities, videos, audio clips, and more!

The AV² Collection

1 Go to www.av2books.com.

2 Enter book code. Y 4 4 6 2 6 3

3 Fuel your imagination online!

www.av2books.com